Grizzly Bears

ABDO
Publishing Company

A Buddy Book
by
Julie Murray

VISIT US AT
www.abdopub.com

Printed in the United States.

Edited by: Christy DeVillier
Contributing Editors: Matt Ray, Michael P. Goecke
Graphic Design: Maria Hosley
Image Research: Deborah Coldiron
Photographs: Corel, Digital Stock, Minden Pictures, Eyewire Inc.

Library of Congress Cataloging-in-Publication Data

Murray, Julie, 1969-
   Grizzly Bears/Julie Murray.
        p. cm. — (Animal kingdom)
   Summary: An introduction to the physical characteristics, habitat, and behavior of grizzly bears.
   ISBN 1-57765-715-2
      1. Grizzly Bear—Juvenile literature. [1. Grizzly bear. 2. Bears.] I. Title. II. Animal kingdom (Edina, Minn.)

QL737.C27 M89 2002
599.784—dc21

                                        2001046441

Contents

Bears

Bears have been around for millions of years. Today, bears are the largest meat-eating, land animals. Three different species, or kinds, of bears live in North America. They are the polar bear, the American black bear, and the brown bear.

Polar Bear

American Black Bear

Brown Bear

Bears are **mammals**. Mammals are born alive instead of hatching from eggs. Female mammals make milk in their bodies to feed their young. Mammals use lungs to breathe air. Most mammals have hair or fur instead of scales or feathers. Apes, dogs, squirrels, whales, and people are mammals, too.

All bears are mammals.

Grizzly Bears

Grizzly bears, or grizzlies, are brown bears. Most of them live in Alaska and Canada. Some grizzlies live in Montana, Washington, Wyoming, and Idaho, too.

It is best to leave grizzly bears alone.

Some people think of grizzlies as wild animals eager to harm others. It is true that grizzlies are wild and strong. Grizzlies may fight to protect their cubs. But these bears are not looking for fights. What grizzlies really want is to be left alone.

What They Look Like

The mighty grizzly is big and strong. These bears have four-inch-long (ten-cm-long) claws and three-inch-long (seven-cm-long) teeth.

Grizzlies can kill with one strike from their clawed paws.

A standing grizzly bear easily towers over people.

Adult grizzly bears can weigh as much as 600 pounds (272 kg). They are three to five feet (one to two m) tall. Standing up on two legs, grizzly bears are 7 to 10 feet (2 to 3 m) tall.

Grizzlies have fur with silver-gray tips. Their fur can be blond, brown, or almost black.

Grizzlies can run 35 mph (56 kph).

The Grizzly Name

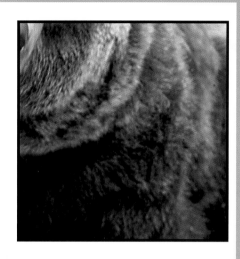

How did the grizzly bear get its name? "Grizzly" comes from the word "grizzle." Grizzle means gray or to sprinkle with gray. And grizzly bears have silver-gray hairs "grizzled" in their fur.

Eating

Grizzly bears eat both plants and animals. Grizzlies eat berries, nuts, grass, roots, and insects. They will eat squirrels, young elk, deer, or caribou. Grizzlies are good at catching fish, too. In the spring and summer, a grizzly bear will eat about 35 pounds (15 kg) of food a day.

Grizzlies fish for salmon and trout.

Hibernation

In the fall, grizzly bears eat a lot. All this food helps them build up a lot of fat. Grizzlies live off this fat during the winter as they **hibernate**.

A hibernating grizzly does not eat. It spends three to seven months sleeping in its **den**. A bear den can be a cave or a hollow log.

In the spring, hibernation ends. Grizzlies will wake up and begin looking for food again.

In the fall, a grizzly bear can eat 100 pounds (45 kg) of food each day!

Bear Cubs

Baby bears are called cubs. Mother bears have their cubs in January or February. Cubs are born in the mother's **den** during her **hibernation**. Mother grizzlies commonly have two cubs at a time. Cubs are small and helpless when they are born. They drink their mother's milk for many months.

A grizzly bear cub.

Cubs leave their **dens** in the spring. The mother grizzly teaches her cubs how to find food. Young grizzlies stay close to their mothers for about two years. Grizzly bears can live to be 16 to 18 years old.

These cubs are learning how to catch fish.

Important Words

den a special, hidden place for bears to hibernate.

hibernate to spend the winter sleeping.

mammal most living things that belong to this special group have hair, give birth to live babies, and make milk to feed their babies.

species living things that are very much alike.

Web Sites

The Bear Den

http://exn.ca/bears/bears.cfm
Learn more about bears and take the
bear quiz.

North American Bear Center

www.bear.org
This site features facts and amazing pictures
of bears.

Brown Bears

www.uas.alaska.edu/uas/wildlife/bearfact.html
Learn what to do if you meet up with a bear in
the wild.

Index